SHOPPING
OR
THE END
OF
TIME

Wisconsin Poetry Series
Sean Bishop and Jesse Lee Kercheval, series editors
Ronald Wallace, founding series editor

SHOPPING
OR
THE END
OF
TIME

EMILY BLUDWORTH DE BARRIOS

The University of Wisconsin Press

Publication of this book has been made possible, in part, through support from the Brittingham Trust.

The University of Wisconsin Press
728 State Street, Suite 443
Madison, Wisconsin 53706
uwpress.wisc.edu

Gray's Inn House, 127 Clerkenwell Road
London EC1R 5DB, United Kingdom
eurospanbookstore.com

Printed in the United States of America
This book may be available in a digital edition.

Library of Congress Cataloging-in-Publication Data

Names: Bludworth de Barrios, Emily, 1983- author.
Title: Shopping, or the end of time / Emily Bludworth de Barrios.
Other titles: Wisconsin poetry series.
Description: Madison, Wisconsin : The University of Wisconsin Press, [2022]
  | Series: Wisconsin poetry series
Identifiers: LCCN 2022013727 | ISBN 9780299340940 (paperback)
Subjects: LCGFT: Poetry.
Classification: LCC PS3602.L833 S56 2022 | DDC 811/.6—dc23/eng/20220419
LC record available at https://lccn.loc.gov/2022013727

For now, these hot days, is the mad blood stirring.

WILLIAM SHAKESPEARE
from *The Tragedy of Romeo and Juliet* (1597)

Moan
into the centuries,
if you can, a last scream: I'm on fire!

VLADIMIR MAYAKOVSKY
from *The Cloud in Trousers* (1915),
translated by Max Hayward and George Reavey (1960)

For Joaquín, Román, and Hera

Contents

SHOPPING
OR
THE END
OF
TIME

RAVINE

Even though we lived at the edge of a great rupture,
It was difficult to tell when the world broke.
For a hundred years our voices (our thoughts) had been connected by long wires.
Then—there weren't any outhouses anymore.
Somebody knew how to make biscuits, light a fire—then they didn't.
I felt so sophisticated all of a sudden, putting store-bought candies in a special
candy dish.
I lacquered my nails.

I had a sweetheart, I was a sweetheart
Somebody's voice was etched into the grooves of a silky black record and at night
and in the afternoon in the golden light of the house I etched that voice into the
contours of my life, songs ran over me like ribbons of silk
There were curtains, and carpets, Formica, polyester, polyurethane
Yesterday I opened a letter from you
I played dominoes with you (creamy quadrangles clacking like bones, fingertips
against the blackened scooped divots)
We bought a one-story ranch-style house
A mimosa tree was covered by its festive pink tassels
Making ice cream on the concrete front stoop (hand-cranking the milk and salt
and egg and vanilla, each of us in turn, a wet stream of condensed water leaking
down the steps)
I captured you in silver molecules (real silver, taken from the earth), silver
arranged in our likenesses on square plates of paper cut with a scalloped edge
The neighbors used to come visit with us,
We went to the moon. . . . .
I kept my lipstick in a special metal case

Your leather blazer, your mustache, your answering machine, your fax machine,
the commercials on TV (My Buddy & Me), your ashtray flecked with gold, your
orange telephone, your pale green chairs and cat, recorded on slide projector
film, your adoration of films, your haircuts. . . . .
We were at the bend.

It was like a shopping mall.

It was like a Baybrook Mall.

Like a landline, like a *69, like a caller ID, like an elaborately intricately lavishly set-designed interior of a store, such an intricate trick that we felt that we were finally entering ourselves, our human inheritance, the glossy dark brown almost black mahogany wood of the furniture sold at the Bombay Company was redolent of the English country manor we thought we probably ought to deserve, the diverse and variegated fragrances and deep green countryside curlicues of Bath & Body Works were like wonderful afternoons eating strawberries out of picnic baskets while sitting on a gingham cloth (afternoons we'd never had)

Then we were wearing all kinds of (synthetic) cloths

We were tugging at our bodies and daubing ourselves with elixirs and then

We loved to write or type long lavish notes to one another, we sent them in the mail, or to each other's email addresses at Hotmail and yahoo dot com

A telephone call sometimes ruptured into a sudden steam of fax machine screeches

My postcards, chosen from a twirling wire rack, written, pored over, postaged, addressed, sent

1-800-506-9511

6159-4931-0135

(The calling card my dad put money on for me to use in high school, the number and the passcode, numbers I remember, used in afternoons to call from pay phones, I didn't have another phone, so convenient to have this calling card number memorized, if I didn't have a quarter)

(Remember now the black receiver, the thick silver cord jointed like an umbilical cord, thick silver buttons, something like an airport, feeling official)

A cell phone. . . . . was convenient. . . . .

Age sex location

To send a little message was a lark. . . .

(In the dark)

I was in bed and my phone made a little noise

You sent some words to me and I read the message in the dark (entire body horizontal)

Makeout Club. . . . . message boards. . . . Livejournal. . . Friendster. . . . .

Some words were unlike the others, they were underlined and glowed a brilliant blue (hot to the touch)

It was senior year at William & Mary

It was 2004

Simultaneously we each received an email inviting us to make an account with a website called (then) thefacebook.com & so we returned to campus, stunned, collectively connected, feeling "seen," feeling the eyes on us

Feeling pricked by the touches of strangers' eyes, everybody knew what we were doing in the dark, our photographs and glowing blogs

(And on postsecret strangers posted secrets)

So in 2008 we put our faces inside our phone.

And anyway a little bit at a time the real world ended

PART 1

—

WOMEN

Part that emerges from a casual sense of ownership

You tell her what the men said, and ask, does this mean I'm
beautiful? What did she say? Try remembering: You are standing
on the corner with your mother. You are standing on the corner.
This pinprick emits no light; it is dark, it is her silence.

Rosa Alcalá, from "You Rode a Loop" (2020)

WHO BEGAT THE EARTH?

Who begat the Earth?   I did.

I grew it three times in my belly.

That isn't true.   It is.

It's a metaphor.   I made three lives.

Who begat the Earth?   Not me.

None of this is my fault.

Who begat the hours that squeeze out like a paste?

God.   What does he look like?   Nobody knows.

He lives in a city.   Nobody knows how to get there anymore.

Who begat the bean vine growing like a slow thought around the trellis?

The Earth.   We inherited it, a palace a mansion a city a forest a ship of treasures we're sinking inside.

80 TO 90 PERCENT OF MY AWARENESS

80 to 90 percent of my awareness
Is a delicate ear turned gently toward my son

Which means I ignore
What would have previously torn me asunder

You may imagine motherhood as a funnel of sand
Into which one is pulled

You may imagine a wrecked ship pulling the inhabitants down with her
Into the water

Except in this metaphor
You are willingly rinsing yourself in sand or heavy water

It is an ecstasy of familial love
Among the sand and water

Whereby you are erased but replaced with something new
Like a new skin or new eyes

And there is a new creature
Sleeping very gently as if in the curl of your ear

Or

Women create people
And that is how humans continue

And that is how women are laid low

Torn asunder
Crippled   Leaking

Etc

Helpless to a helpless thing

Threads of feeling and attention
Binding or sewn

Women lavish their attention

Women lavish their emotion and then
They do not have some left

History is a 6,000-year block
Inside which women are torn asunder

Picture yourself in a room with smooth white walls
(No windows no doors)

That is the myth of motherhood

It says motherhood may be a perpetual caring
Or a gradual erasing of the self

Or a sacred blanket
Or a devastating failure

To be a mother
Is to be a figure in a painting

Wrapped in a sacred blanket

Whatever the observer sees
You, the woman in the painting, you turn your head and continue

Being already busied with sheltering your small companion
Into the course of his life

WHEN I WAS 13 THERE WAS A GIRL I KNEW

When I was 13 there was a girl I knew and an awful thing had been done to her

For three weeks the whole school stopped

One of my teachers wrote a poem about it and read it to our class

The feeling of the poem did not match the horrible thing that had happened

The poem was like an artificial flower in a vase

It gave you that feeling

Which is not to say the teacher was not sincere

But the feeling of the poem did not match the holiness, or the sanctity, or the sadness, or grief, of what had been done

There was a space around what had happened, filled with water, density, or void

You couldn't get near it

MY GRAVESTONE

My gravestone   I mean my grandmother

is standing in heaven looking back at me   I mean

her body is mouldering in a coffin in the cemetery

Her heat energy having dissipated in however many seconds

My grandmother   The other one   Mouldering on a hospital cot

with a head that aches and lungs full of fluid

How would you mourn for someone who's rotten?   You don't

You do   For example I have a collection of glimmers of the person she could
have been

if she had had a different father   One sliver:

her lush lovingly green attended-to highly productive garden

In a memory the ping of shelled beans drops into a metal pot

If it made a difference Johnnie I'd be wishing you sweet sleep

THE MOTHER SHOULD BE AS STUNNING

The mother should be as stunning as an angel dripping with pure water

Putting little sliced pieces of herself in her children's lunch boxes

she cuts herself into the shapes of orange slices and Ritz crackers

portioned out into Ziploc bags   At the library   In the park   On the sofa

Women   made of pure water   offer kisses at sundown

Shutting the bedroom door feels like   a form of anger   a form

of abuse   to firmly clip the threads that tether me to them

I think of the ducklings who love their mother in a pond   Their ardor

in a straight line   And desperation to be near her   In the myth

Gaia is the mother of the first gods   She's also the Earth

When her children finally spring away from her   (out from her)

it's the beginning of time   The gods arrive on the surface of Earth

and begin to be alive to their own wisdom   I'm alive

inside my children's eyes   No   I'm the surface upon which their days unfurl

WITH PLEASURE THE YOUNG MEN

With pleasure the young men   dismantle the young women

With pleasure their sick slick grins drip over the wet idea

of humiliated flesh   When a woman dyes her hair

When a woman has her hair dyed   or chemically straightened

or chemically permed   there are searing singing singeing thorns

as the edges of the scalp burn   A damp blunt scent   A wrong scent

A blonde scent   An odor like a mistake was made   Only a dope

would slather herself in such an odor   A beautiful dope   A beautiful

door   At the steps of the mall we entered to transcend

Who could really transcend   the words of young men

Wet T-shirt contest   Fingering   Titties   Whore

INITIALLY I WAS A BEAUTIFUL WOMAN

Initially I was a beautiful woman   Then I wasn't

Time   dismantled me

Initially I was a baby   Then a handful of freckles

lying flat on my chest with a book   My gold-framed glasses

covered in fingerprints   Why did I wear a smile?

I didn't know about this world

Initially I was knotting a friendship bracelet for years in the 4th grade

Don't look at me   in a hallway lined with lockers

Not even a handful of good words   A culture

kisses my forehead and presses me into the pages of a magazine

Tumbling out into the cosmetics aisle of the pharmacy

I opened a clamshell compact   What a miniature door!   At the gates

someone could have described the cost

A NAKED WOMAN IS PERCHED IN THE WINDOW

A naked woman is perched in the window

A naked woman made of porcelain is perched

Her left hand placed on her chest   Looking down and to the left

as if to say   *No thank you*   As if to say   *Enough*

I've had enough of this life   Having remained fixed long enough

Hair blown back   like wind from the sea   Gold paint is

a pretty fire burning at the temples and neck   Women are for

long strong thighs   Creamy skin covering its muscles

Enough   It's leaving soon   It's leaving now

And taking itself somewhere away from us   Taking herself to the sea

THE DOVES WERE MOANING CRYING COOING CALLING

The doves were moaning crying cooing calling

Inside their houses the people were moaning crying cooing calling

A damp hot air   A person shouldn't be allowed to write a poem

kept cool in a cake of conditioned air

What are your opinions?   A person might be proud of their opinions

Like polishing ordinary rocks and collecting them in a box

Some advice: Or not

I take off the voice of a prophet

I sink my opinions into the sea

What sound is there now in the hot damp world?

Some advice: *Who cares*   say the shaggy globes of white clover

Who cares sing the doves   *Who cares* says the damp blunt air

boiling with the odor of our choices

A MAP IS A PICTURE THAT SHOWS WHERE THINGS ARE

A map is a picture that shows where things are
I am here, lying sideways on linen sheets (legs stretched in cool sheets)
(Black-dark house, black-dark night, quiet crickets, quiet freeway)
You are there (thumb sliding across the screen, hand resting guilelessly on a
mouse, fingertips floating and caressing a rectangle of mouse, hands handling the
paper pages of a book, a papery quadrangle, a hexahedron of paper stacked and
splayed apart)
You are there (feeling impartiality, or impatience, or disgust, really incisive
judging thoughts coursing freely through you)
You're there (feeling fine, feeling caught within a swiftly moving current)
I am here (in the past   Time extinguishes itself immediately)
(Like wet fingertips pressed   Like a wet singe   Like a flame that has a squeezed
fat gasping belly
Time immediately puts itself out)

Time extinguishes itself immediately
Time vanished and left behind a landscape still containing people and cars but
not the same people and cars
The day always finds itself awaking in the remnants of the past
The rubble of last night's dishes, the evidence of decisions
You arrived here having inherited all your decisions

The world is a layer of decisions that have accumulated for 10,000 years
I have arrived here among the ingenuity of the world
(Among sewn coats and the idea of ancient breakfasts preserved in paint carefully
dabbed upon canvas)
Like some sheaves of papers slipped into the thinnest cracks between boards,
We have arrived in the world where poems have been secreted among the years
So yes this miracle exists
We arrived in a world where so many of the magical papers (bearing poems)
survived
And even now we can leach their magic through our eyes

PART 2

—

MONEY

Part that drifts in the air from the Ship Channel

After 3 days of rain
They look like lakes
These fields near Hockley
fields waiting for cotton
Corn or soy
Tract homes or condominiums
Or little malls
Glimmering like fish-scales in the sun
As a sheet of egrets settles in
beside the lakes
That will not be here
in three days
In fields that will not be here
in three years

Lorenzo Thomas
from "Equinox" (2004)

MY HUSBAND FIDGETS WITH THE INNER MECHANISM OF THE COUNTRY

My husband fidgets with the inner mechanism of the country

By which I mean he works inside a financial institution

Like a man inside a gray metal factory or tinkering in the bowels of a deep ship

By which I mean he makes the country work

And which you probably think is cruel, evil, selfish, insulated, or unconscionable

To which I would suggest that you are ignorant of the way reality functions

To which I would say someone invests in something and that is how it comes to pass

For example vaccines vehicles fuel supply fresh produce

But many suffer you say   It is not fair that many suffer

It is like a suffocating damp helplessness placed onto the throat

Yes I would say   The road we travel is cruel and many suffer

The suffering is unfair and not noble

It's a frozen thing that's dead and cannot be thrown away

THE CULTURE ORIENTED ITSELF TOWARD SHOPPING

The
Culture oriented itself toward shopping

The culture
Invented a flat vivid world to sink into

As one sinks into a bath and closes the door and runs the warm water with a

Book
Or a glass of sharp wine

Inside
The white noise of water out rushes any immediate concern

Some lives have been scrubbed of immediate concerns
Or mud
Or weather

After work
Some shopping

For work
Some shopping

Running to the store
And picking up some food

Or
Hiring a contractor

Or
Someone for the lawn

Purchasing new clothes

Which
Might confer some attractiveness and dignity

Materials
Which could convey

One's
Inner goodness, attractiveness, and taste

Having the best qualities and correct values

Best thoughts
Are elaborately patterned

Worst thoughts
Rise up as a self-righteous ego, scarlet and furious and fuming into fingers

Or alternatively as a sheet of empty area

Wherever the personality goes when the activity ceases

When it is neither buying nor preparing for a future purchase

In the car
The environment is leather and black and smooth sweet odor

Serenity
Is composed of quality materials

It has contours which are a pleasure to take note of

As the wishes rear up

On the way to or from some shopping

A little appetite leaks out

So obvious in fact
It need never be discussed

A feeling of perpetual lack

Is the water in the river we float down

I flow from the lip of one day
To the next

As if lounging on a cool dark river that's

Composed
Of what I might purchase

In the mall
The stores are horizontally stacked

Into discrete dioramas
Of hypothetical lives

I sample the hypothetical lives

I unwrap them
From the quality tissue paper and boxy bags with hard sharp creases

Black
And gold and pink and peacock blue

I imagine
There is a certain kind of person somewhere

Who wears these clothes with grace

A person could exist who carries grace in their chest like a warm affectionate
orb

I've expected to eventually become

I've been on the verge really of emerging into grace and ease

Kindness
Effortlessness

I like to be among the

Everybody
Is carrying the fierce fire of their souls

Hid with some intentional or inadvertent packaging

IN MY CHILDHOOD

In my childhood   insects leave pieces of themselves

everywhere   Spherical eggs on a leaf   Moth cocoon

with exit hole   (Papery and brown)   The papery

circles of a wasps' nest   Architecture held by a

thin stem   Webs   Dense as cotton wads   Spread

like an elegant hand   Ripped   Or holding drops

of water   A cicada skin with a slit in the back

See-through   (A complicated yellowing window)   A wax

honeycomb suspended in a jar of honey   Gather

what we are fond of   Exterminate the remainder

In my childhood   I gather what I'm fond of

at 1221 Merriewood Dr.   4.06 miles from the Brio Superfund Site

Declared on March 31, 1989   4½ months before

I entered kindergarten   to learn to read my way

(one day) through a Wikipedia page listing the toxins:

copper, vinyl chloride, 1,1,2-trichloroethane,

fluorene, styrene, ethylbenzene, toluene

Satisfying diagrams show how the molecules fit

Pink color, orange color, blue color CH_3

C_6H_6 I admire how a scientist puts a comma

in the middle of a word   I like how he hangs a small

number under a letter   Red color, purple color

Hoops and stars   "Aromatic hydrocarbons"

"Known human carcinogen"   Opening a door on my memory

So-and-so's wide blue eyes   His brother's wide brown eyes

"I'm a Brio kid," he says, meaning   *We lived in the*

contamination zone   and   Health studies shuttered

due to low participation   Yearly packets of money

for the remainder of your lives   The child carries

the mutation and the man dies   It's bucolic

where they razed the houses   Somehow it's legal

for cows to graze on it   A host of pretty wildflowers

Luxuriant luscious grasses nodding their broad

shaggy heads   At sunset hordes of bats pour

from under the bridge at Dixie Farm and Beamer

In the dark a longhorn lifts and turns his burdensome head

In my childhood I   the refinery operates from 1957 to 1982

"unprocessed petroleum and waste materials"   "12 large earthen pits"

"groundwater"   In my childhood I scramble out from

the creek water   spooling   brown   opaque   and placid

Hiding something, maybe   An alligator or a snake

Clambering out through the mud and sludge

Dangling from a large pipe of some type   A patch of

wilderness   among the strip malls and asphalt

Green light   green trees   I gather a doll-sized bouquet

of clover   A roly-poly pools in my palm   In my childhood

insects leave pieces of themselves   emissaries from

a natural world   Many fewer each year

We could not live in peace   Laying out pipes and lines

and cement roadways and houses weighing many

thousands of pounds   In my childhood

we entered the tunnels of the future   Emissaries

from a dwindling world   Searching for an

entrance to get back to   through tainted sludge and water

THE ECONOMY IS SYNCHRONIZED AND DELICATE

The economy
Is synchronized and delicate

Or

It is robust

Like a red wine
Or a flavor of coffee beans clipped in a brown paper bag

Something sort of expensive
And shipped over the sea

For which to satisfy
Our complex and robust hungers

Robust could describe a young man in a painting
Cutting swathes of wheat with a scythe

In a field that is gold and yellow
It is the wheat and the late sun

The light falls in "pools" and "slants"

It is the 19th century
In my hypothetical painting

His delicate white shirt is damp with sweat

It is nice to believe
That his mind is smoother or simple

Like a passageway painted white

In a more primitive town

Before the economy got to be so sinuous
And having such long delicate fingers

The economy lies
Lightly or tightly

On the Earth
Like a wreath

It's a loosely connected network

The barges carry the containers
Which transport the boxes

Which hold the things
Across the Earth

It is a type of sorcery
Or it is a highly organized delivery system

Deriving energy from various nodes
Made of persons and products and types of desires which sprout or languish

Deriving energy also from desperation, actual need, also from longing which
may be laid out languidly or casually
Like an outfit across a bed

Desperation like an intense and immediate need for food

Desire meaning to imagine oneself golden, wire-thin, very cool, or interesting
On an intensely blue water or an intensely white beach glaring against white
sand

The economy
Like a perfectly conditioned person

May seem temporarily
To be robust or "just right"

Like a person laying out in just the right climate
Heavily upon some warm sand

I live
Among the economy

In a brick house

I open the things
And I throw away the plastic

For as long as I'm able
This will be a pristine household

With crisp and cool conditioned air
With water that runs from the taps

And outside still some wild harmless animals

A falcon or a hawk
A swarm of a hundred maybe delicate and nonaggressive bees

A slender snake
A dozen newly grown toads

Packages from Amazon arriving every other day
The freeway alive with a hundred thousand cars

Thriving into the city

The economy causes a man to suffer robustly
Or a woman to profit so that joy creeps throughout her life

Delicately
Like a familiar face suffused with warmth

From the refrigerator
She removes the delicate foods

In a house that is cool
In a yard that is picturesque and safe

IN THIS HOUSE WE LOVED

In this house we loved   We broke into the light and/or out into the dawn

We were like a movie   We were not like a movie   Too much

or too many of our stories are shown to us   on a flat screen

They are flat stories   like a stock photo that shows a man and a woman

grinning or laughing widely   making breakfast pancakes and the man

with no shirt and the woman wearing the man's discarded shirt

I would be nervous to be in a situation like that   To be so gorgeous

and to be so uproarious   (in that perpetual state)

They sit down to breakfast then and their delicious words

squeeze out into a paste   in the bright house filled with the

bright light of morning   (As if love were a perpetual garland

       ringing out over beautifully photographed landscapes)

MY DARKEST THOUGHTS

My darkest thoughts are like dipping a United States into a scabbard.

A United States flexes itself on a map   What was it like

to grow up inside the hegemony?   Nothing special of course

What was it like to live inside that economy that pressed you into

a flattened portion of a person?   It wasn't so dramatic, we were okay

My childhood is a museum display of the suburbs in the 1990s

Behind glass: a trampoline, a fax machine, the memorized telephone numbers
of my friends

What fruits had you eaten as a child?

Only banana watermelon Red Delicious apples and (very expensive)
strawberries as a treat

More often it was the idea of fruit, something flavored like a fruit

Strawberry Pop Tart.   What's inside it?   A deep red smear of sugar

As red as.   Oh I don't know.   A smear of emotion

What was it like to grow up inside the hegemony?

On the one hand the nation was swinging its head and stamping its hooves

On the other hand we were eating what they told us was food, we believed
them forever

It was food   We knew what they told us was true

IN THE MIDDLE OF THE DISASTER NOTHING BAD
HAD HAPPENED TO ME

In the middle of the disaster   nothing bad had happened to me

What do Cairo, Houston, and Caracas have in common?

I was like a plastic nougat   petrochemicals smeared all over me

Cheerful fires off-gassing   Cheerful plumes of smoke pumping up

in the atmosphere   Don't laugh   The mall was like a diamond

I don't care if you believe me   Back then we believed in the

power of our perfect money   The sound of the word dollar was like

a lollipop lolling around in our mouths   Can't you feel it, too?

First my father   then my husband   using machinery to extract

oil up from the earth   Come out come out   Up from the ocean shelf

The Permian Basin   The North Sea   Off the shore of   And off the shore of

And on the shores of the world's deepest lake   In Russia Alaska Australia

Venezuela Louisiana Egypt   In one part of the Sahara is an ancient graveyard

filled with fossilized bones of ancient whales   Architecture of
ribs   Architecture

of ancient life you can stand inside   (But you can never be a slab of ancient

whale gliding through a pure ocean)   (Ancient ocean encrusted with mussels as if with diamonds)　　In the Texas Hill Country　　100 million years ago

an ocean sifted gently　　Another ancient dried-up ocean　　Hiking I found

a stone mollusk　　And a second mollusk　　Then a mollusk as big as my
hand　　Dizzy

in a column of 100 million years　　100 million years is a long tall
column　　What lasts?

In March, 36 thousand gallons of drilling fluid were leaked into the rock
formation

beneath the Blanco River　　"Oops"　　The Trinity Aquifer　　Well-water

thick as milk, and brown with slurry　　The shores of time　　The ocean erodes
time

Gently sloshing　　First my grandfathers　　Then my father　　Then

my husband　　Tending the machines that convert one form of petroleum

to another　　Off-gassing a torch into the night sky

Towing a chemical barge into the Ship Channel　　That grim gray

city-like stretch of pipes and points and pure-white domes　　How do you
build

an oil pipeline across the ocean floor?　　I don't know, but my father knows

(Once in 1994 he brought home a tape of film from the sea floor. . . . .

the mouth of the pump. . . . . . artificial light in the complete dark. . . . . .

nothing. . . . . nothing. . . . . a large fish. . . . . . particles. . . . . . vastly salty, empty, and wet

And the machinery and the secret filth spilling out. . . .)   The mall was like a diamond

Ritualistically on our 13th birthdays our mothers took us to the manicure salon

Hold my hand   Massage my fingers   Moisten clip sand lacquer

The special chemicals made in the vats   (nail polish remover made from toluene)

(the same chemical that burned in the ITC chemical fire)   (a dark plume that lasts for days)

(alerts the public to their secret filth)   On our 13th birthdays   And biweekly thereafter

Clear gloss   A crescent moon   Off-white ends   "A French manicure" is what I typically picked

Or a clear colorful varnish which shone like a rainbow in the light   (like oil in a puddle)

(I think of the firemen who don special suits to enter the chemical fires)

(I think of the women who work in a boxy room   in a strip mall breathing solvents

Scrubbing solvents from their skin   after dipping each of my fingers into a small white vat)

The mall was like a diamond   An atrium of glass   Like a well-appointed cage

The stores trafficked in the most convincing lies. . . . . . .   Here you will be an
explorer. . . .

Here an apothecary. . . . . .   Sail down the Amazon River and shake a rain
stick. . . .

Shake a rain stick. . . .   What is that exactly?   Nobody knows   Didn't you
love

the Bombay Company?   Almost black, lacquered look of expensive
mahogany wood

Unapologetically   in those gushing years   we wanted to look expensive and
correct

It wasn't a fashion of goodness, morality, fairness, or justice   The stores

were like plotlines of a book   We were the main characters   It was as if

we were in the midst of doing glamorous things   or emotional things

We were imagining ourselves characters   living some meaningful lives

What we wanted then was glamour   campy glamour, or a glamourized
version

of our ordinary lives   Nowadays people have more particular tastes

All the time humankind growing more wise and less wise   A length of string

manipulated into different shapes   Back then we believed in the power

of our perfect money and the veracity of our perfect lives

What do Cairo, Houston, and Caracas have in common?   Looking around you now

what can you touch that does not contain oil?

They say   oil is the remains of ancient organisms   They say oil is the fault of big companies

or maybe we should recycle better, and more   The government fingers its unwritten regulations

like a terrible moral failing   Seeds the future with microscopic particles of plastic

In the middle of a disaster   nothing bad had happened to me

The mall was like a diamond   What can I touch that does not contain oil?

First my grandfathers   Then my father   Then my husband   with phone calls

casting invisible strings across the world   casting lines between the numbers

in this bank and the numbers in that bank   Lines   pumps   drill bits   sunk costs

fixed costs   acreage   The geologist who loves deep time   manipulates the program

makes a map and a graph and shows the investors where to use the new technology

"Fracturing bedrock formations"   Like a terrible moral failing   Whose?

MY NEW BLUE KITCHEN CABINETS PAINTED BLUE

My new blue kitchen cabinets painted blue
Black countertops, black granite flecked with dirty starlight
And saltillo tile from Saltillo, Mexico, baked, glazed earth and still some little
imprints from the foot of a dog who passed probably 50 years ago
When the Earth had fewer dogs probably but more species, fewer people, but
more thick forest, more dark trees and the webs strung between the trees,
clumps of sticks pushed into nests with the vulnerable blue, white, or cream
eggs inside, speckled, warm, the squirrels' nests that contain two entrances
that are also two exits, a burrow in the sky, warm and dry
A bird singing with its narrow throat, its voice a slender stem
The legs of the insects slender as stems
The stems numerous and dense moving in quick ticks
My thoughts numerous and dense
Thickly sprouting, dumb

Reading the *Appendix to the Journals of the House of Representatives of New
Zealand. Session I.*, 1884

H. B. Sterndale to Hon. J. Vogel, "concerning the resources of the greater
number of those islands of the Pacific upon which I have at any time resided or
with which I have been engaged in trade"

> "Beginning with the dark hour just before dawn, the stars are
> shining with an intense brilliancy, reflected on the steel-bright
> surface of the calm lagoon. The sandy pathways seem like snow.
> The heavy forest of towering palms and banyans, interlocked with
> trailing vines, assumes weird and fantastic shapes, and shows a black
> outline against the clear blue sky; under their dark shadows twinkle
> innumerable points of light—the lamps of great glow-worms and
> luminous grubs."

. . . . reading and relishing (as Sterndale was writing and relishing)
the precise prose used to describe what could be plundered, what could be

eaten, what could be taken, what could be converted into such a thing that it could be transformed (like melted tortoise shell or chopped and canned bêche-de-mer), shipped, sold and bought, several times over, until it found a resting place with a creature in a far part of the world intent upon bringing what is lush, vibrant, and tasteful into her home

IS THE WIND SO DIRTY?

Is the wind so dirty?   Wiping down Román's rocking horse

that was left out on the porch   Punch-bright yellow plastic

under a slim scrim of mottled black dirt

Ah   Air spills in from the Gulf   I don't want to talk about

the Ship Channel anymore   Even though it looks like the Emerald City

if the Emerald City   were aluminum-colored and anodized gray

Cylinders and cream domes   "Flaring" is what it's called   to blaze the "upsets"

An emergency of hydrocarbons   (Exquisite-looking)

(Gemstone of fire the size of a room)   In her book

Economic Growth versus the Environment:

The Politics of Wealth, Health and Air Pollution   Dr. Judith A. Cherni describes

Houston's monitoring sites   smelting of metallic ores

(Then) "1200 hazardous installations operate along the 25-mile channel"

"The odour of ozone resembles, in fact, the 'smell of the air after a summer storm'"

Today the sky is either   sapphire or lapis lazuli

I won't talk about it anymore   I don't want to talk about it

anymore   Xylene   benzene   toluene   and naphtha

OUR HOUSE (AMONG ALL THE HOMES IN THE CITY)

Our house (among all the homes in the city)
Is like a ship
And I say that because it is filled with white light
And is surrounded by a rumble of white noise that feels quiet
Like how wind must feel on the water
(With the police siren going   with the interminable freeway sounds)
(An eternal wind blowing)
Our house stands expansive and expensive
On our street where there's also a sex motel, apartments, rental properties,
mansions, demolished mansions that are now a blank space, tall skinny
townhomes built to fill every blank space, a megachurch like a megalodon
dominates half the block
This is the city we made together collectively by accident
Nobody agreed to it
Nobody meant it

Our house (among all the homes in the city)
Is rimmed with camellias which withstand the bitten frozen bitter nights
Thickened glossy sturdy leaves and blowsy round voluminous blossoms
Everybody loves a garden and a row of flowers
A fence of beauty
Our house like a poisonous mirror
Stand on the sidewalk and peer at our house
It will reflect back upon you your own inadequacies
It will make you feel safe
Like this is a safe neighborhood where somebody cares and methodically
engages in a regimen of maintenance   Tilling the soil with fertilizer and
bending at the waist to pluck weeds up by the root   An interminable
vigilance to pluck problems up by the root
Take care lest you become a problem

Our house (among all the homes in the city)
Did not flood

It rose above the floodwaters

Which were a brown clouded mirror   A glossy mirror   A liquid sky vibrant
with live oak leaves bunched and crowded   The water like an oil painting
vibrant with detail

Our house which rises eight feet above the street

A mammoth resting on orange clay dredged from Brays Bayou which used to
wind like a lithe serpent and used to offer life to herons and snakes and a dairy
farm was thriving where our house and all the other houses are now built up

Goodbye to that bayou and those cows and herons and the crawfish

Brays Bayou is a drainage ditch and concrete-lined culvert

It holds the water when the sky's too full with it and the land's too full with it

Its banks are concrete pavement gray and man-sized drainage pipes open onto it
(What's missing is the color green)

To walk along the bayou (which flooded the city, which saved the city from
flooding)

Is to walk among the city that men made

Which is a gently pitched angle of industrial gray

I think there is a universal law that one thing or many things must always be
sacrificed for another to thrive

PART 3

CHILDREN

Part in which eyes grin, arms swat, little mouths speak

At this time there are few
poems about pregnancy and childbirth
do I find this curious
I want to shriek at
any identity
this culture gives me claw it to
pieces; has nothing to
do with me or
my baby and never will,
has never perceived a
human being.

Alice Notley
from "A Baby Is Born Out of a
White Owl's Forehead—1972" (1998)

A GHOST IS WHAT YOU CALL A WOMAN

A ghost is what you call a woman
Who has three children in quick succession
Smiling in a garden of children
The woman lies down on the soil
She is now a witch
A witch produces magic in the world
I chop apples
I chop chunks of cheese
Three pieces of magic dot the house
Joaquín, a piece of nature
Román, a sliver of adventure
Hera, squirming like a creature at the bottom of a well
Who goes there?
Light filters through the forest leaves
The birds ate all the bread
Quick, turn the page
The witch chops chunks of cheese
The witch mixes butter into the pasta
Places the plates on the placemats
Twists the cap from the frosty milk
A ghost animates her body
Her body is dotted with minute holes
Out of which she streams in minute pieces
Her soul
Like cool wind
Skirts around the bodies of her children
On the wind her soul is carried away from her
A woman made of wind
Blends into the shapes of the house
The house like a woman is a series of shapes
Bent into spaces to hold you

THE NEW MOTHERS

The new mothers   were bitterly shocked   because no one

had told them   Fold up your youth and put it away

Fold up your time   Fold up your bladder and your waist

Fold up your face   Sweep your hair into the trash

Fallen gestures   Dispirited flags   The new mothers

soaking through their sheets   Cold at midnight   The new mothers

with their bellies   cut or split open   After the swelling

music   I couldn't walk myself to the bathroom yet   The night nurse

paused on her way out   "Your baby's awake"   My responsibility now

THE UNBEARABLE CAN ACTUALLY BE BORNE

The unbearable can actually be borne

The birthing book says
The abdominal wall might split in half

The perineum may need to be split
And breasts are really not

As society tells us
Designed for sex appeal and pleasure

So it does not matter what they look like after

An additional thing I give birth to
Is a setting down of vanity

Which feels like a rod of burnt or frosted pain

Setting down one's vanity
One no longer carries the burden of it

Imagine your youth as a frosted plate
And you drop it and it splits in pieces

So now it is broken
You can clean it away and continue

MY PREGNANCY WAS A LONG AND HAPPY NIGHTMARE

My pregnancy
Was a long and happy nightmare

During which I ate
Pint-sized tubs of ice cream and walked around the block

Becoming more tubby and unwieldy
As if living in the skin of a drum

Wielding and propelling my belly
Feeling dreamy and druggy in the suburbs under the sun

I walked around the block
And watched episodes of *The Twilight Zone*

In 1960s America
It was silver and gray and all the people had disappeared

The tick of a clock
Rang out

Men spoke in voices that were
Urgent and clipped

Women languished in the oppressive heat
Of a wet, dying sun

In *The Twilight Zone* the world was always
Dying

In our imaginations
The world always dies

Drowned or burned or infected or
Contaminated out

By imagining a death so huge
Hoping to infuse our daily lives with sweetness or urgency by contrast

The world dies
How sweet is this morning

The world dies
How urgent my life

There is a belief that life
Should be spent leaning forward as if squinting into a bracing wind

As if life's juice or marrow or interior liquid
Can be drained or squeezed or sucked

If the world dies I hope it will be
A cinematic death

A beautiful woman
Laying down in green grass in a dewy forest

A golden gray mob tearing itself apart,
Full of great emotion

When the world dies I would prefer it to be
Without disappointment, shame, or regret

Shame hangs on a man's neck
Like a terrible bell

Joaquín when he arrived arrived
With no shame upon him

Instead he carries a sweetness or urgency
Inside him

For example he is pleased
With the bath's warm water

He is pleased with his
Small naked body

The world when he looks out across it
Is a field of universal truths

It sways or rings with
Unplucked truth

NOTHING COULD BE SWEETER THAN

Nothing could be sweeter than   Joaquín in

a yellow coat   Or Román in red shorts   Or Hera

in a purple hat   Or Román in his sleeveless aquamarine

beach tank   Or Hera in her lime-green body suit   Or

Joaquín in his flamingo-pink tennis shoes

Or Román telling himself a quiet story   Or Joaquín

putting his shoes back into the shoe cabinet   Or Hera

performing the slow deliberate abdominal curl to roll herself over

Joaquín announcing   "Hera smells like blueberries and the color of evening"

Román wanting to be a horse   His perception of something

Strong   graceful   talented   and gentle

After watching *Black Beauty* he declares   "I'm Beauty"

Román returning from the bathroom   "I'm handsome

Me   I looked at myself with my black eyes"

Román   "You scared?   I'll go with you brother"

Then one boy isn't careful with the other

Then they're yelping and complaining

Then Hera's face curls into pain   Then Joaquín is frustrated to get his turn

Then Román wants the pink plate but doesn't get it

Then he wants cubes of watermelon but the cubes aren't perfect cubes

Then Román can't calm down

Amid the rushing purple water he sees himself within the torrent

Amid rushing shudders   "I can't calm down"

Román discerning himself among the rapids   My favorite miracle today

JOAQUÍN IS MY FAVORITE CHILD

Joaquín is my favorite child   And Román is my

favorite child   And Hera is my favorite child

She emanates the aura of a garden   Román

describes his emotions all the time   Joaquín finds the books

in the science section   in order to decipher the world

"I want to learn about volcanoes"   In the index "V"

"Volcanoes"   Page 61   Molten rock spewing   Glowing orange

Such things occur on Earth   And moray eels who are chartreuse

A hammerhead   its eyes mounted on lateral stalks

Someone said   Your children's childhoods are for you

They won't remember them   Sifting flour into the bowl

In miniature chef hats   Adding very ripe bananas

Does every generation hope   this next one can resolve the world

STATUES OR KNOTTED ROPES OR SCORED STONE

Statues or knotted ropes or scored stone or magnetic tapes or marked paper or
grooved plastic or painted fibers or braided filaments
Are devices for storing information across time

A person is a device
For storing information across time

The parent melts or dissolves
And up springs the child

A person

Is a phenomenal device
That assembles itself from dirt and air

The Greek gods of ancient history
And the Sumerian gods of ancient history

Glisten
In the distance at the far edge of time

With familiar shoulders elbows ears and eyes

Their crisp or frail emotions
Coursing down like cobwebs or hair

Triumphant
Is how it feels

To enter the river of human history

Parents

May drizzle a warm sweet attitude
When discussing their handsome children

Having replicated myself
Personhood will reassemble in my children

I could desiccate and die
Having assembled some children

I ASK JOAQUÍN IF HE LIKES THE MUSIC

I ask Joaquín if he likes the music I play for him each night

Joaquín says Piraí Vaca's classical guitar is "ghost music"

The room at night   is filled with the eyes of ghosts

Plastic stars fixed on the ceiling   Piraí Vaca

plucks his guitar and drops the notes   Water

becomes glossy with light

                              The room made into a box of evening

And in a distant distant distant city the Piraí River exists

Or   the river passes through the city   renewing itself

like a mind composing itself again in every fresh moment

The room is a box filled with sparks staining the air

Ghosts startle from Piraí Vaca's soul   leaning over the water

Joaquín one day these nights will be a ghost that leans out toward you

ANDRÉS SAID

Andrés said maybe we could grab that baby back.

From out of my bloodstream.

I'd heard on the radio that the mother carries the cells from each of her pregnancies in her blood.   Until she dies.

That was when Andrés named him Aquiles.

He had already been gone two years by then, flushed from the uterus, already since a new child had grown there, sweet as a flower.

In the bloodstream, Aquiles, a permanently wilted flower, circulating even now, ever since.

The miscarriage is a child who lives in the minds of the mother and the father.

A little sweet ache common as water.

Each kindergarten class padded out with five or six extra ghosts.

WOE WAS THE SENTIMENT

Woe was the sentiment on
everybody's tongues as they
lugged their bodies (face to phone) past
children in pajamas hugging good morning   past bathroom sinks   past
oranges, eggs, coffee   past trees (green chlorophyll winking like ancient
     dreams)   past the brittle electrified scent of ozone simmering   past other
mothers unlatching children from car seat straps . . . .
Everyone it seemed was sad as I welcomed

Hera into my arms in the hospital bed as Dr. S sewed me back together and
everyone was
reeling with the news of fresh
atrocities and

tragedies, eternal tragedies covering the Earth and atrocities small as the gem
     mounted in a ring and carried everywhere
one goes. . . . .   Someone was bereft

over money   someone felt lonely   someone felt
ugly, inside and out   and I
rolled Hera into a smoothly wrapped blanket and I wondered what will one day

please and vex her   What complexly
laced thoughts will she drop like
a garland on top of the soil   What woe   Hypothetically ideally she will
never
experience
the queasy uneasiness, instability, pain, sorrow, and discomfort the people of

Earth have claimed
as their perpetual inheritance   Ideally she will blossom as a
rose or a camellia blossoms,
teeming, joyous,
heady, quick, avid, eternal, permanent   She'll always be happy, and she'll live
     for all time

PART 4

GHOSTS

Part that is approaching the end, The End, some endings

Oh you who are alive on Earth, . . .
I speak to you of what happened to me . . .

from the inscriptions of the
Tomb of Petosiris (ca. 350–330 BCE)

SITTING AT THE LIP OF THE TUNNEL TO THE PAST

Sitting at the lip of the tunnel to the past

I want to ask my grandmother about her childhood all the time

Ssssssssip   That portal is closed

That span of time is being carried further back behind us

Both my grandmothers always had a vegetable garden

I think they didn't want to starve

We ate well during the Depression, Gandy said   (with pride)

Her mother made biscuits on a wood-burning stove

Lunch was a biscuit wrapped in a cloth

What did you notice at night, is a question I would like to ask

What were you afraid of   What kind of bugs were there

What kind of games

I drive my head into the tunnel   Below my pretty image of

crickets in a navy-blue night   an intolerable sound of not anything

IT IS SAD

It is sad
That your thoughts don't mean much

Like how a movie theater
Projects colored lights into your head

And afterwards
In the bathroom

Face to face with yourself over the sink

That's still you
In the grim and gray reality over the sink

Crumpled popcorn smeared into the carpet

The colored lights in your thoughts
Soaring

Like a very advanced camera
Photographing mountains or clouds

Also it is sad
When your brilliant mind has nothing of substance to settle upon

Like a high schooler
In the suburbs

Thinking complicated thoughts about lip gloss

A complicated web of mascara, and glossy magazines, and one particular boy

It is sad
When the brilliant thoughts look cheap or brittle in the light of day

It is a little embarrassing
To recognize your thoughts as cheap or brittle in the light of day

Some brittle thoughts
In the crisp light of morning

It is sad
When the thoughts that breathe in you

Gloriously

Wither and escape

As evidence having left just a faint whisper of smoke
Or an eminent or auspicious feeling

It is sad to have been abandoned
By your own brilliant thoughts

They well up in you and then are gone
You are composed of 100,000 slivers

Welling up and then gone

WHAT IS YOUR IDEAL LIFE

What is your ideal life
What can you do to achieve it
(If you are reading this with your eyes you will notice that I have omitted the
question marks)
(Why did you leave out the question marks)
(I desired a flat deadpan tone a cynical curved twist of the paring knife)
(Totally predictable and tonally bereft of depth)
(Atonal cynicism bereft even of covetousness no sharp deep inhale of jealousy
and vicious desire like a heedless headlong gasp)
What shape is your desire
A mumble
How are you going to achieve it
A puddle
(Broad flat cool nonactive reflective of the sky)
Start again
What shape is your desire
An apple (tight skin, a variety of very pretty colors)
What shape is your desire
An afternoon or morning (shapeless, ungraspable, of utmost importance, then
missing, unalterably, for infinity and for all time, muffled in our brains for a little
while like cloud descended to the street, walking through and among its tufts)
What shape is your desire
My children's little hands that want to hold my own (little hands that grow older
and then old)
What shape is your desire
To be purple, fog-white, fuchsia, amethyst, rose, gold, ribbons of palm-frond-
green fluttering in a thick wet wind rushing in from Galveston
What shape is your desire
Words in the air, words on a screen
What shape is your desire
A letter in a shoebox on sale at a garage sale (somebody's desire and thoughts
preserved in a box)
What shape is your desire
The books   which manage to contain   the fluttering world

I AM GOING TO MAKE A POEM

I am going to make a poem

As if
I could put beautiful things in a box to keep them there

It will contain
Freeway sounds and the bayou which is pinned right to a straight line with its
concrete sides and slab

(In the past it used to wind)

(I'm going to wind toward the park along the concrete pavement path along
the bayou's concrete bank)

(Some animals have managed to survive by staying mostly out of sight)

My poem will contain
One large swamp rabbit (who is eating birdseed from a birdfeeder's base)

Holes in the ground that are a burrow or a nest

A heron, or that type of bird that stands in water and hunts

White blackberry flowers (everywhere white on spiky purplish green, a net of
future food)

The blue blue bluebonnets planted by the city, improbably blue

The struggling undazzling humility wildflowers unsanctioned and unplanted
(a little dirty white cup, a small shining glossy yellow)

There's a freeway sound and a helicopter sound and a field of unbroken
crickets who I think are bleating or singing or otherwise crying out

(They cease their cry when I walk by)

(Man destroys the world and spring still happens)

(I make a jagged poem
To put the remnants in)

WE EACH OF US CARRY

We each of us carry the murder
Back with us into our houses apartments or townhomes

There to unwrap it and inspect it

To shake it gently, it makes no
Sound

It is our murder now and we
Have it in our kitchens

It is a thing that grows without
Growing

It creeps or spreads or slides
Down the block turns the streets and seeps out further

Eventually through the whole
Neighborhood until we all have it

Each of us some portion

Meanwhile it remains mute
Dumb and stupid like a stone

Look for yourself it's hard dumb
And stupid   A dense stupid stone

I carry with me a dense stupid
Stone

You are curious about the details

I will not share the details

I take out the murder-stone

I wait on it

It does not produce aphorisms

I picture the murder-stone in
Other people's houses or apartments or townhomes

I wonder which aphorisms are
Sliding out of their murder-stones

Smart knowledge sliding out like
Thin strips of typed-on paper

What meaningful observations
Are occurring in other people's households

They I hope have the talent to
Bring life or meaning to the murder-stone

The murder-spot is an invisible
Energy that continues to rock

That continues to disappear

That continues to ruminate in the
Kitchens families homes

A death or a murder disappears
Eventually

It becomes a story

Best-case scenario the people left
Standing make it into a story with some type of good

And eventually they put it to rest
So they or it can rest

Eventually into history and into
The ground

Best-case scenario it disappears

And doesn't continue to pulsate
Like an invisible energy or a weighting pain or an ongoing fear or a persistent
and inscrutable stone

NEPTUNE IS A PLACE WE'LL NEVER GO

Neptune is a place we'll never go

Even in a spacecraft and even
Protected from the vacuum of space

And the methane or whatever it is
There and etc

We'll never enter its blue light

Never crossing the many black miles

Even our descendants will never go there

Never energetically planning

And packing
For a fantastical journey into outer space

Never to unify
Into a jaunty, better mankind

Inside a well-crafted, windowed hull

Peeping out to the wide planet or stars
Which loom gigantically in the window

I speak now directly to the descendants

Who will also never travel
The solar system or beyond

Descendants

If you are reading this
Many years will have passed

Mine is a realistic and ancient voice

You
Sadly have not united

Into one stupendous mankind

You are still like us

Disparate and greedy

Not having defied the odds or
Conquered the dismal emotions

Lying in the dead, cold graves on
Earth

Probably still you pine for the
Fantastical humans

Who unite into a striving, better
Mankind

Please continue to kindle them or
Dream them

The fleet of jaunty selves who unite

And set out together from Earth

Who coordinate
Our badge of future honor

In an organized and smiling fleet

ALL THE TIME ART IS FALLING

All the time art is falling

out of people's eyes   On the living room wall a painting of

a girl blowing a bubble of pink bubble gum   Squinting off

the way a person does when they are mulling   The artist (Alejandra

Delgado) has painted and scratched monsters into the white paint

around the girl's head   Eyeless or dead monsters / Meant to show

the sweet child has / Everybody is / People have gold locked inside them

If gold is a substance made of thousands of landscapes / different monsters /

fragrances and I can't / can still remember / The monsters are emerging

from the lake again / That lake is the cold teardrops

saved up from your history / It's the cold teardrops of

anger / discontent / time slipping backwards past your

fingertips / what you should have done better, etc

This exquisite wind and sun will pass / I will pass

Majestic memories jut up from the horizon / There your childhood self

is collecting freckles / Your motherhood self is trailing

up and down the stairs at midnight   patting a baby's back

The teardrops lap against the shore / With time they've gotten heavy with wisdom

You are becoming so laden with wisdom

The weight of it is like falling asleep in the snow

The weight lends wisdom to your eyes

The art is the same art you looked at before

Only now it conveys the weight or wisdom of the world

I have gold locked inside me / It's the kisses Joaquín placed on my palms

IT IS TURBULENT TO BE A PERSON

It is turbulent
To be a person

Filled with wishes

To say "I want"
Amid the swarm of desires

Being emitted
Across the Earth

It is redundant
And it is self-important

Let us try it now

I want a trampoline

I want to tramp
Loudly throughout the house

I want to trample upon the achievements
Of mine enemies

Who wrong me with each
Innocuous success

Through our desires
We come to know ourselves

Meaning
Your desires could confirm

The nature of your values

Eg, a man may wish
To be seen as powerful

A woman
Might want to be seen to be pretty

Or a person may want to be
Left alone all day to watch the shows

And eat something
Really salty or delicately balanced

A person may want to remain in the warm pool of bed
A little longer

Or to create something
Very meaningful

To live her life as an elegant experiment

Also to have
Effusive thoughts

Also and etc

Desire pecks at every person like a shadow
It is his great companion

In a swarm of desires
We are overcome

We are confused or overwhelmed
By their numerous branches

We lay down as if to die or sleep
In a thicket of desires

Having stumbled in a thicket
Of shadowy desires

One desire chooses us for a favorite

It stings our lips

If we are lucky
One desire stings our lips

And beckons us toward life

HYPOTHETICAL PAINTING

(for Dorothy in the dark)

This still life is of a vase of flowers
The flowers are the ordinary, small, dirty-white clover you can find growing on
the side of a municipal path, on a patch of soccer field, in an unmown meadow,
in a yard
The humble whitish flowers are shaped like a globe and are visited by bees
(honey bees)
This handful of humble globes has been arranged in an antique vase
It is Depression Glass, Art Deco, triumphant, a little bit of dime-store glamour
Fluted, triumvirate legs, trumpet-shaped mouth, Grecian, clear singing
green. . . . . .

(This vase once belonged to some lady, maybe wearing a cotton poplin dress,
Maybe listening to the radio sing *You Oughta Be in Pictures*
While she was soaking something or wiping something down,
Having arranged in the thrillingly elegant vase a scraggly bouquet
Picked from the fields or the ditches,
Somebody living through a deep depths of this country's poverty,
When we were almost universally collectively saving coffee tins,
Washing and preserving used foil,
Butchering our own hogs, cleaning the intestine,
Mending what broke, running away from home, getting run out of our homes,
Soaking a bed-bug mattress in gasoline, doing homework by kerosene,
Lunch was a biscuit wrapped in a cloth,
Taking pride in eating well, if we could eat well,
Splurging only rarely maybe never on a tube of lipstick yards of fabric a pretty
vase. . . . . . .)

This painting takes place at night, in the dark
The only lighting is ambient, chilly, city light
Filtering in through the skylights and adjacent windows. . . . .
Even in the little light

Dimples of the table's oak glistening

The clover's odd, thin, upturned petals, weak and tender without their plant and roots

The glass glowing sharply like pieces of ice. . . .

This is a subtle, humble painting

It's meant to convey a feeling about the past

Which is continuously leaking out behind us, streaming away

In that way

It contains a message that, in only a few years, can be properly interpreted by no one

This painting is trying to remember what it was like

It is intended as a gift for those who can remember what it was like,

Which already is almost practically no one

Acknowledgments

A number of the poems from this manuscript were published in the chapbook *Women, Money, Children, Ghosts* (Sixth Finch, 2016). "My pregnancy was a long and happy nightmare" was reprinted in *jubilat*'s Emergency Issue, no. 30.5 (January 2017). "My darkest thoughts" was featured on *Poetry Daily*, September 22, 2020.

…

Acknowledgments are due to the editors of the following publications in which some of these poems first appeared: *Annotations, B O D Y, Carve, Cincinnati Review, Columbia Journal,* Electric Literature's *The Commuter, Harvard Review, Jellyfish, Magma, Oxford Poetry, The Poetry Review,* and *Sixth Finch.*

Wisconsin Poetry Series
Sean Bishop and Jesse Lee Kercheval, series editors
Ronald Wallace, founding series editor

(B) = Winner of the Brittingham Prize in Poetry
(FP) = Winner of the Felix Pollak Prize in Poetry
(4L) = Winner of the Four Lakes Prize in Poetry